crochet

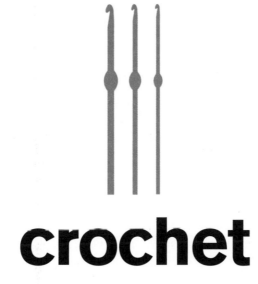

crochet

20 projects for friends to make

super+super

First published 2015 by
Guild of Master Craftsman Publications Ltd
Castle Place, 166 High Street, Lewes,
East Sussex, BN7 1XU, United Kingdom

ISBN 978 1 86108 736 2

A catalogue record for this book is available from the
British Library.

Publisher: Jonathan Bailey
Production Manager: Jim Bulley
Senior Project Editor: Wendy McAngus
Editor: Nicola Hodgson
Pattern Checker: Jude Roust
Managing Art Editor: Gilda Pacitti
Art Editor: Rebecca Mothersole
Designer: Simon Goggin
Illustrator: Anna-Kaisa Jormanainen
Photographers: Rebecca Mothersole, Claire Culley
and Harry Watts

Set in Akzid, Ani Lazy Day and Calibri
Colour origination by GMC Reprographics
Printed and bound in China

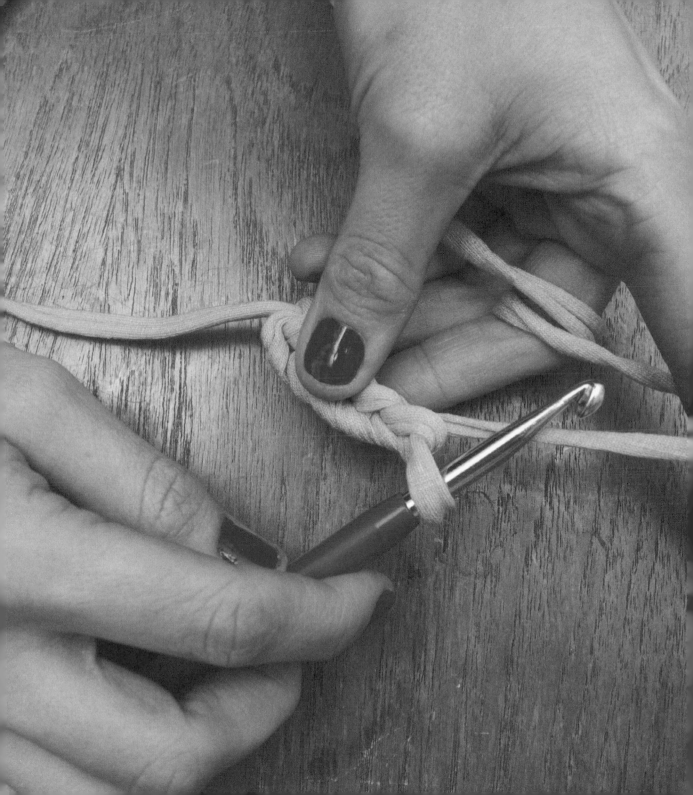

contents

Introduction to crochet

When most people think of crochet, they think of the slightly scratchy blanket on their grandma's bed, the oversized tea cosy their mum has had for years, or that dodgy sleeveless cardigan their dad wore in the 1970s. We have those memories too, except we think about how awesome they were and wonder: 'Where could that go in my flat? You can never have too many blankets, right?'

Crochet's current rise in popularity has meant we are now taking this retro practice and mixing it up to create contemporary homewares, on-trend accessories and fun gifts. Through the use of different types of yarn, cool colourways and various techniques you can start to build your own crochet personality. You don't need a fancy pattern to make an effective piece of textile design – the joy of crochet comes from its simplicity and in experimenting as you grasp the basics.

The term 'crochet' comes from the old French word 'croc', meaning 'hook'. Crochet hooks can be made from nearly anything, including carved bone, wood, cast metal, plastic or bamboo. This age-old craft essentially involves pulling loops of yarn through other loops of yarn with a hook to create stitches in rows or in the round. One great thing about crochet is that, unlike with knitting, only one stitch is active at a time so you need not worry about dropping a stitch and laddering your piece. If you make a mistake, you can simply unravel your project a single stitch at a time to get back to the point where you can rescue it.

Much like the recent resurgence in hand knitting, crochet is finding its cool on public transport (and it's far easier to work with a small hook than with two pointy needles while commuting), at Stitch 'n' Bitch crafty gatherings, and as urban art in the form of yarn bombing. If you've not seen yarn bombing where you live, it is basically graffiti made with beautifully coloured, lovingly crafted pieces. Once you have learnt a few tricks from this book we highly recommend you take to the streets and have a go yourself!

Amy & Claire, Super+Super

Get in the loop!

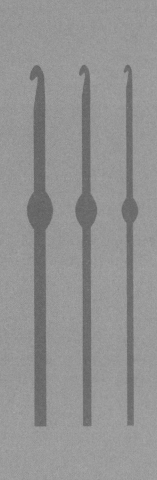

...·*(!)*·...

ready, steady, make

Using this book

Like other books in this series, this book is a collection of 20 projects of varying difficulty. Throughout the book we encourage you to personalise each project, for example by choosing your own colour of yarn or by adding a pompom or a fancy trim to take your design to the next level.

Each project aims to build up your crochet skills while increasing your confidence and making lots of lovely homewares and accessories at the same time. Every project is perfect for a gift or to keep for yourself. By the end of this book you will be a crochet master and will be ready to tackle different types of crochet and more complex patterns.

The book is divided into four sections based on how long and involved the projects are. This means you can make sure you have enough time to finish a project before you start.

Lazy Crafter
These projects are ideal for absolute beginners and will give you maximum impact for the time and effort invested.

Weeknight Winners
These projects are short enough to be completed in a single evening and can be made with items that are readily found around a crafter's home. They are ideal for an evening in alone or to make with a group of friends at a crafty get-together.

Perpetual Creative
These medium-length projects will keep you inspired over a quiet weekend (or two) when you need a creative intermission in a hectic working week.

Committed Crafter
These longer, more complex, projects can be enjoyed at your leisure over an extended period of time, while on holiday or sabbatical. They are great for improving your confidence and expanding your skills base.

The wonderful thing about crochet is that you can do it wherever you are – on your sofa, in the park or during your commute. If you have somewhere comfortable to sit and your bag of kit to hand, you can be a mobile crafter. Some of the projects can be quite time-consuming, so take regular breaks to rest those wrists and eyes.

Try starting with the Lazy Crafter projects to get to grips with holding your hook and practising the basic stitches. Once you feel comfortable with these, you could get some pals over and tackle some of the Weeknight Winners or Perpetual Creative projects – you can help each other if you get stuck. Don't worry if you make mistakes; just pull on the yarn to unravel the stitches back to the point where you can try again.

Before long you'll be tackling the Committed Crafter projects with ease. Crochet is very rewarding, and you'll relish dedicating your time to creating your own crochet masterpieces. Once you have built up your confidence, try the techniques you've learnt to make other homewares. Try your hand at making a granny square blanket or use those crochet-in-the-round skills to make yourself (or a newborn) a beanie hat.

What you'll need

The great thing about crochet is that you only need a few basic pieces of equipment to get started. Most of these things can be picked up fairly cheaply from a craft shop or online, and if you buy your yarns in bulk you can always get a bargain.

hooks and other equipment

1 Crochet hooks

Crochet hooks come in a wide range of sizes. For the projects in this book you'll need 4mm (UK8:USG/6), 6mm (UK4:USJ/10) and 9mm (UK00:USM/13) hooks. Bear in mind that UK and US crochet hook sizes and stitch terms are different. In this book we use UK sizes and terms, but in the future you might pick up a US pattern and be confused. Fear not: there are plenty of online resources and tables to help you translate your pattern accurately.

2 Tapestry needle

You'll need a needle with an eye large enough to thread yarn through to sew in the ends to complete a finished crochet piece. Opt for a needle with a larger eye so you can thread the yarn comfortably.

3 Embroidery needle

Embroidery needles are great for appliquéing onto your crochet designs. Choose the best size to accommodate the yarn you are going to stitch with and make sure it has a pointy end.

4 Scissors

For this book you will need only a basic pair of craft scissors. No need for anything expensive – even your kitchen scissors will do just fine.

5 Embroidery thread

Use embroidery thread with your embroidery needle to personalise your work or to appliqué a cool design.

6 Mini craft pompoms

These synthetic pompoms are ideal for bringing a bit of joy and colour to your crochet designs.

7 Toy stuffing

A little bit of toy stuffing is great for padding out designs or filling pieces. We've used it to make the Squishy Wrist Rest for your workspace (see page 82).

8 Measuring tape

Always keep a measuring tape to hand to measure lengths, check tension or to make sure your design is the desired size.

9 Plastic press poppers

We've used plastic press poppers for the neckpiece on our bow tie design. These are easy to use and simple to attach.

10 Snips

If you are crocheting on the go, keep some snips in your bag. They are ideal for snipping ends and are smaller than scissors so are a great space saver.

11 Felt

Felt is great for making placemats and coasters. Buy the thick variety from your local craft store.

12 Pompom maker

Some of the projects in this book require you to make your own large pompoms. These makers ensure you can whip one up in no time.

yarns

We use lots of different types of yarn in this book: from cottons to T-shirt yarns, we like to mix it up. Some people get confused between the terms 'wool' and 'yarn': wool is the fibre from a sheep that is used to make a woollen yarn. Yarn is basically anything you can crochet or knit with, encompassing a huge variety of fibres from bamboo, silk and alpaca (natural fibres) to viscose, jersey and acrylic (manmade fibres).

Yarn for crochet is sold in balls or skeins, but often also comes in spools or cones. Skeins and balls are usually sold with a label or yarn band printed with care instructions, weight, dye lot, suggested hook size, likely gauge, fibre content and tension, including how many stitches to expect per length of fabric made.

Balls and skeins of yarn are generally sold as 50g or 100g. Cones are more likely to be sold in 250g or 500g weights and are more expensive; you can order them from yarn manufacturers (they are generally not sold in haberdashery departments). However, look out for bargain cones of yarn in charity shops or car boot fairs. They are perfect for larger projects such as blankets and cardigans.

Traditionally, crochet items were made in crochet cotton. This was usually mercerised, which means the cotton fibre is twisted in such a way when it is spun that the finish is shiny and smooth. Crochet cotton also comes as brushed cotton, whereby the surface of the fibre is roughed up to give a more matte and scratchy look and feel. A little more rustic, perhaps!

1 Fingering weight yarn (4-ply)
The gauge of a yarn is the thickness to which the strand of yarn is spun. This gauge is used for socks and lighter-weight projects such as baby clothes. We use it for our Chic String Shopper (see page 96) with a 4mm (UK8:USG/6) hook (larger than you would usually use with this weight of yarn) to create an open, lacy look.

2 Double Knit or DK yarn (8-ply)
DK is the most commonly used gauge of yarn in both crochet and knitting, and is widely available from craft shops and haberdashery stores. This type of yarn is most commonly used with a 4mm (UK8:USG/6) hook. We use it for projects including the Tassel Tie Bunting (see page 36) and the Fancy Tote Bag (see page 38).

3 Chunky yarn (12-/16-ply)
Perfect for snuggly mittens and cosy winter hats, this yarn crochets up quickly due to its thickness, which also makes its extra sturdy for homeware projects like the Teatime Tea Cosy (see page 78) and the Squishy Wrist Rest (see page 82). Chunky yarn is most readily available in a wool/acrylic mix. This yarn combines the warmth of a natural fibre with the strength and durability of a manmade fibre. We generally use this yarn with a 6mm (UK4:USJ/10) hook.

4 T-shirt/jersey yarn
This is made from long lengths or strips of T-shirt fabric and is often composed of mixed fibres such as a cotton and viscose blend. This is a thick yarn and we usually use it with a 9mm (UK00:USM/13) hook. It is great for high-impact homewares such as the Chunky Pouffe (see page 92) and the Vino Holder (see page 110).

Tip! The dye lot number identifies the different batches of yarn manufacture. Always buy enough yarn for your project from the same dye lot to avoid running out and having to buy some more from a different batch, which might be a slightly different shade.

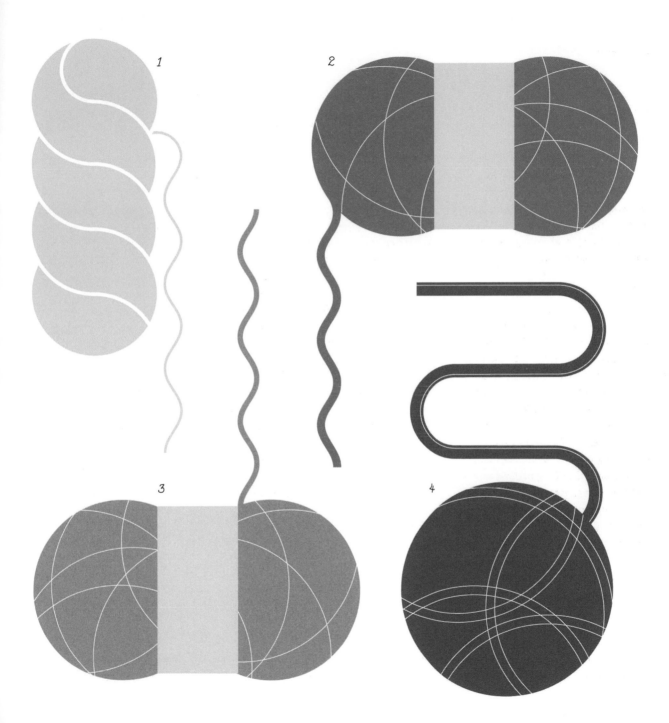

How to do it

Use this handy guide for information on how to make the basic crochet stitches. You may find it a little awkward at first, but the stitches are easy to memorise and you will soon be crafting!

Holding your hook

Although this comes down to preference and whether you are left- or right-handed, you would generally hold the hook between your thumb and first finger, with the hook end nearest your fingertips and the rest of the hook length under your palm, fingers gently curling around it. However, some people prefer to hold their hook like a pen. You will soon find what feels most comfortable.

Slip knot

1   Make a full-circle loop with your yarn.

2   Using your hook, pull the long end through its centre.

3   Hold the short end as you draw the knot tight.

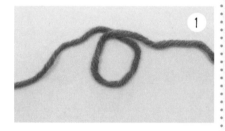

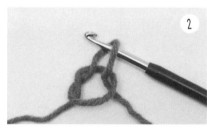

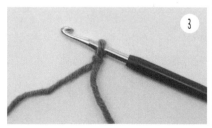

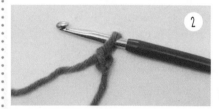

Chain stitch (ch)

This is the most common foundation row for any project worked in rows.

1   Make a slip knot and place it on your hook. Pull this small enough to feel secure on your hook while still allowing for movement left to right. Now wrap your yarn over the hook towards you.

2   Catch the yarn with the end of your hook and pull this through the slip knot to make a second loop.

3   Repeat this yoh (yarn over hook) and drawing through with a steady tension and watch as you create a long length of chain stitches.

Double crochet (dc)

There are two parts to a double crochet stitch (abbreviated to 'dc' in patterns).

1 Push your yarn into the stitch space with your loop securely on your hook.

2 Wrap the yarn over the hook towards you and pull the yarn through towards you. You will now have two loops on your hook.

3 Wrap your yoh towards you again and draw this through the first and second (all) loops on your hook.

Treble (tr)

A simple way to get a treble (abbreviated to 'tr' in patterns) right is to remember that you have to wrap your yoh *before* you pick up your row or push it through into the stitch space.

1 With your loop securely on your hook wrap, yoh towards you.

2 Insert your hook into the row (at the third chain along if working the first tr of the row). You will now have two loops on your hook.

3 Wrap the yarn over the hook again.

4 Draw through so you have three loops on hook and yoh again.

5 Draw through the first two loops so you have two loops on the hook.

6 Now yoh a second time. Draw through the remaining two loops so you have with one loop on the hook.

Turning chain (tch)

This is the extra chain stitch (or stitches) that you make at the end of a row (when working in rows only) to keep the edges neat and the row changes even. Your turning chain will always be the same height as the stitch you are working. Therefore, double crochet (dc) needs one chain stitch for the turning chain; half double crochet (hdc) needs two chain stitches, and trebles (tr) need three. The steps below represent the turning chain for a dc.

1   Once you reach the end of your row, make your last stitch as normal.

2   Wrap yoh.

3   Draw through to leave one loop on your hook.

4   Turn your piece round so it is facing the direction in which you will continue crocheting.

5   Push your hook into the next stitch space as shown. Then yoh and draw through (two loops now on hook).

6   Yoh and draw through (two loops now on hook).

7   You've now successfully turned and made your first dc stitch. Continue along the row as normal.

Slip stitch (sl st)

This stitch is most commonly used for one of two purposes: to join crochet together when working in the round, or to join in a new colour when changing yarn colour. Here we show the steps for changing colours.

1   Begin by making a slip knot in your new colour.

2   Push your hook through the area needing to be joined and place your slip knot onto your hook.

3   Pull the hook back through as shown.

4   Wrap yoh.

5   Pull through. You are now ready to continue with the new colour.

Making a centre ring

This is when you work your stitches in a circle (in an anti-clockwise direction) around a central point.

1   Start by making 5 ch.

2   Push your hook into the first stitch.

3   Sl st to join and form your circle.

You can now work into this circle going forward.

Cluster

A cluster is when you crochet several stitches consecutively into the same stitch space but finish each of them at the top before you start the next stitch. This way they fan out at the top and stay together at the bottom. A good example of this is a granny square (see the Granny Square Stool Cover, page 102).

1 In the picture you can see an example of a first cluster in the corner of a granny square already made.

2 After making a chain stitch to create the corner of your square, start by wrapping yoh and pushing the hook back through the same hole you have already worked into.

3 Pull through to leave three loops on the hook.

4 Wrap yoh and pull through one loop, leaving two loops on the hook.

5 Wrap yoh and pull through the last two loops.

6 Repeat the same process with another treble stitch.

7 Make your final treble into the corner. You'll notice how all the stitches have pulled around to make the corner.

Working into back loop only to create a ridge

Several of the projects, including the Neon Tablet Case (see page 70), require you to work into the back loop only to create a ridge. This can be achieved using any stitch; we use dc in this example. This technique creates a distinct front and back.

In this sample, we pick up our pattern a few rows in, and we have used different colours to show the method more clearly. First make the correct number of chain stitches for your project and crochet the first row in the chosen stitch.

1 In your next row (Row 2) you will work into the back/wrong side of your ridged crochet work to create texture on the front/right side. You pick up the back loop of your dc stitch (the closest stitch to you) and crochet your stitch.

2 Work the whole row, working into the back loop only of your work.

3 The back of your crochet should remain flat...

4 ...and the front should be appear to be ridged.

5 Make your turning chain and continue to the next row.

6 On your next row you will pick up the front loop of your stitch (that's the one furthest away from you) as the right side is now facing. Work in this way to the end of the row.

7 To achieve the ridged effect, keep alternating this method. You will begin to see a flat (back) side and a textured, ridged (front) side.

Casting off

This is how we finish our work to make sure no snipped yarn ends unravel.

1 To cast off, begin by snipping your length of yarn as shown.

2 Wrap yoh.

3 Pull the short end through.

4 Continue pulling through until the yarn pulls through completely. Hey presto, a secure little knot has been formed.

Sewing in ends

You can either weave ends in with your hook to secure them or you can use a wool needle and sew in an over stitch. We show you both methods so you can use whichever you prefer.

1 To sew in ends, begin by threading the yarn onto your needle.

2 Push the needle to pick up one part of a stitch as shown.

3 Repeat this process again with another stitch. We do this to make sure it is secure and won't unravel later.

4 Pull through and cut down with your scissors.

5 Voilà! A neat finished product. We do this not only to neaten the back of the fabric but also to secure the cast-off ends.

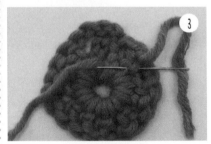

Crocheting in ends

1 When crocheting in your yarn ends, start by making sure the ends are neat and facing the direction you are going in.

2 Place your hook into the next stitch.

3 Continue with your desired stitch, making sure you are making it over the loose ends.

4 Continue along your row, covering the ends more with each stitch you make.

5 Carry on until the ends are completely covered.

Japanese foundation row

This technique involves crocheting into the back/wrong side of your row of chain stitches to create a finished edge at the start as well as at the end. We use this for the Chic String Shopper (see page 96).

1 Turn over your chain to reveal the back (or wrong side).

2 Pick up the next stitch with your hook ready to carry on crocheting.

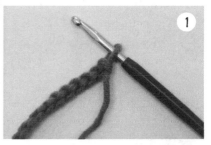

Finishing touches

Sometimes simple crochet stitches are all you need to make an eye-catching accessory or colourful gift. However, at other times you'll want to go to town with some extra embellishments. Here are a few ideas for going that extra mile.

Making a pompom

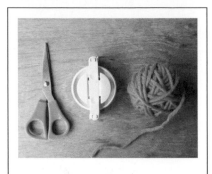

WHAT YOU NEED

- ☐ Pompom maker
- ☐ Scissors
- ☐ Yarn

Tip! The more yarn you wrap onto your pompom maker, the neater and fuller your finished pompom will be!

1 Pull one leg of your pompom maker out and start wrapping the yarn around the leg. Try to wrap away from you.

2 Once the first leg has a chunky layer of yarn on it, push the leg closed.

3 Pull out the second leg of your pompom maker.

4 Wrap the yarn around the second leg in the same way as the first. Make sure it's a nice thick layer.

5 Close the second leg, making sure both sides have an even amount of yarn on each side.

6 Take your scissors and, holding the flat white circular centrepiece, snip around the entire edge of the maker.

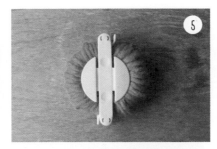

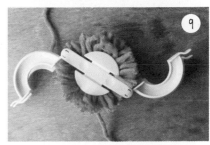

7   Cut a length of your pompom yarn about 6in (15cm) long, ready to tie your pompom. Wrap this around the cut edges of the pompom maker.

8   Make sure your yarn sits in the grooves where the two sides of the maker fit together. Pull this tightly and tie in a double knot to secure.

9   Now your pompom has been tied, pull both legs out to the sides ready to remove your pompom.

10 Lift off the top plastic section of the maker by pulling the circle up. You've pulled the legs out so it should come off easily!

11 Repeat this on the other side to reveal your finished, slightly misshapen, pompom.

12 Roll your pompom around in your hands and fluff it up to its full glory. Leave the two lengths you used to tie its centre to attach your finished pompom to your project.

Blanket stitch

This stitch was traditionally used around the edges of heavy wool blankets to reinforce them and stop them from fraying. We use blanket stitch on the Fancy Tote Bag (see page 38) and the Shell-trim Placemats (see page 56) to create a foundation on which to work crochet stitches.

1 Starting with your threaded needle, tie a knot in the end and come up at the edge of your fabric, from the back of your work to the right side.

2 Push your needle into the fabric a little way along and loop your yarn around and under the needle at the edge before you pull it through.

3 Repeat this a little distance along the fabric to form three sides of a square.

4 Repeat this along the length of the piece(s) of fabric you are working on, keeping your tension even.

5 Fasten off securely on the wrong side of your project.

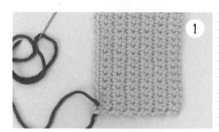
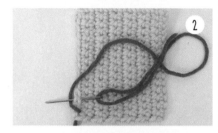
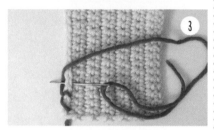

Chain stitch

This is a decorative surface stitch that creates a lovely loopy pattern. We used it to embellish the Appliquéd Pot Holder (see page 60).

1 Make sure you cut extra yarn for this stitch as it uses double the amount of other embroidery stitches.

2 Starting with your threaded needle, come up from the back of your work to the right side.

3 Loop your yarn around clockwise and push your needle back into the fabric next to where you came up to start. Move forward out of the fabric again, wrapping the yarn behind the needle as it pops through and trapping it.

4 Pull your yarn through and tighten the loop around the length of yarn.

5 Sew through the centre of the first loop to the right-hand side of where your second stitch came up through the fabric.

6 Pull your yarn firmly to create a second even stitch.

7 Continue this method all the way along the length of your fabric until your desired pattern is complete, then fasten off at the back.

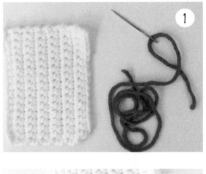

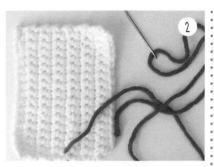

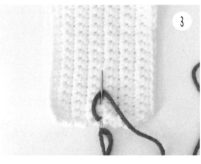

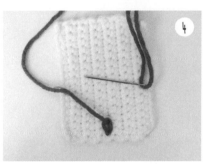

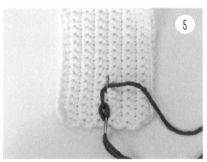

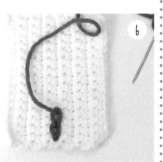

Running stitch

This is a great stitch for tacking pieces together while you work or as a decorative topstitch.

1 With your threaded needle, come up from the back of the work to the front.

2 Now, depending on the length of stitch you want, push your needle back down through the fabric ¼in (6mm) in front of where you came up and pull your yarn through firmly.

3 Continue sewing in a wave-like motion up and down through your fabric with an even stitch length until you reach the end. Finish the yarn neatly on the back of the work.

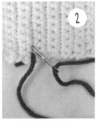

Tension

Tension refers to how loose or tight your crochet is, and consequently how loose or tight the feel of your finished fabric. Everybody's tension is different. A tight tension results in more stitches per length, whereas loose tension results in fewer stitches in the same length.

Achieving the correct tension, as given in the pattern instructions, means that the size of your finished garment or item will match the size stated in the pattern. The thickness of your yarn will alter the tension of your crochet, so always pick the correct sized hook to match your yarn and use the gauge of yarn specified in the pattern.

In the pattern instructions, tension is stated as the number of stitches and rows there are to a given measurement, usually 2in (5cm).

1 To make a tension swatch, make a square of crochet in the stitch you will be using for your project. Use the right yarn and the stated hook size.

2 Once you have made up a square, use two pins to mark out 2in (5cm) along a row for the stitch count.

3 Then mark out 2in (5cm) down for the row count. You now count how many stitches there are inside this 2in (5cm) space, and usually double it to find how many per 4in (10cm) there are. Check this against your pattern. If you have more stitches than required, your tension is loose, so try again with a smaller hook. If you have fewer stitches than required, your tension is tight, so try again with a larger hook.

Mattress stitch

This stitch is used to achieve a high level of finish to a project. It allows you to sew perfectly matched seams that are also invisible. Your finished stitches should look like a row of ladder rungs until you draw them together neatly at the end.

1 To start, line up your two pieces next to each other with right sides facing up towards you. Make sure that all rows are level, with rows 1, 2 and 3 on the right-hand piece matching up exactly with rows 1, 2 and 3 on the left-hand piece. You need to pick up the same part of the stitch each time to achieve evenness and you will work from the bottom to the top of your pieces.

2 With a threaded needle, bring your yarn up through the bottom right-hand corner stitch (back to front) and pull it up till it stops.

3 Now bring your needle down (front to back) through the stitch on the left-hand piece that is its direct parallel. Pull the yarn through until you have a ¼in (6mm) length of yarn bridging the two pieces.

4 Bring your needle up through the same row but slightly forward – your needle and yarn are now at the top of your crochet piece.

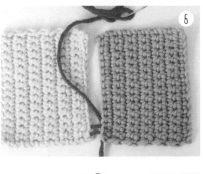
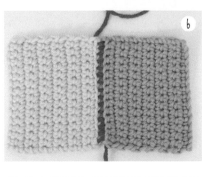

5 Take your needle back to the right-hand piece and sew through the edge of the fabric directly opposite your last stitch.

6 You will be able to see a row of ladder-like stitches starting to bridge the gap between the two pieces. Continue working from right to left, then left to right in this systematic way until you reach the top of your work, finishing with your yarn and needle on the right.

7 Now with your left hand steadying the pieces, pull your yarn gently up and away from your work, drawing the ladder stitches together like a zip.

8 Your finished mattress-stitched pieces should show no signs of stitching and the join should be very neat.

Oversewing

This stitch is somewhat like a diagonal running stitch; it can be used to join pieces, as a decorative stitch, or to secure ends.

1 Lay your two pieces flat on top of each other, right sides together and lining up edges neatly.

2 With your threaded needle, sew from right to left through both pieces, finishing this first stitch with your needle on the left.

3 Bring your needle around the front of your work and back through the right-hand piece to the left, sewing both sides together in a circular stitching motion. Your stitches will be parallel.

4 Repeat this method, sewing over and over and pulling your stitch securely each time. When you get to the end, sew off neatly.

Blocking

Blocking is an important finishing touch to set pieces into their desired shape. Pin your finished pattern pieces into shape on a padded blocking board or ironing board. Once you have gently steam ironed your pieces, leave them on your board and only remove when completely cool.

Following patterns

The thought of working from a pattern can sometimes be daunting, but don't worry – they're there to help! Once you have got to grips with the basics such as making a tension square, practising stitches and remembering their names, you will soon get the hang of it.

Every good pattern should come with set parts to help you master your new craft. These include:

• A list of the tools and equipment you will need to complete the project, including the type of yarn and size of crochet hook.

• The size of the finished item so you know what to aim for.

• Tension measurements detailing the number of stitches and rows you need to achieve.

• A guide to any special abbreviations or techniques used.

Patterns are written using abbreviations for the stitch names for brevity. See right for a list of the abbreviations used in this book.

The best way to use a pattern is to start at the beginning and master the basics. Learn the stitches and make a few wonky squares. Get to know your natural tension, and whether you are a tight or a loose crocheter. Once you feel you have made some progress with the first steps, take a look at the patterns. Choose a quick, simple project that inspires you and contains some of the techniques you feel confident in. Now go for it! Read over the pattern a few times and take it step by step, looking at the pictures. Annotate a step if you get stuck so you know what you need help with.

Our last piece of advice is to take regular breaks: there's no need to get stressed out, especially at the start! If you get confused, mark your page, put the kettle on, and give your eyes and fingers a rest. If your hands and wrists feel tense or sore when you first start, try stretching. Interlock your fingers and push your hands inside out away from you.

Abbreviations

Crochet patterns are usually written using abbreviations of the most common terms to save space. These terms may look alien and confusing at first, but refer back to this page for an explanation of any abbreviation you are unfamiliar with.

3ch	chain of 3 stitches
beg	beginning
CC	contrast colour
ch	chain
ch sp	chain space
cl	cluster
cont	continue
dc	double crochet
MC	main colour
rep	repeat
sl	slip
sl st	slip stitch
st	stitch
st sp	stitch space
tr	treble
yoh	yarn over hook (more often than not towards you)
to	repeat the section of pattern between the first * and the last *

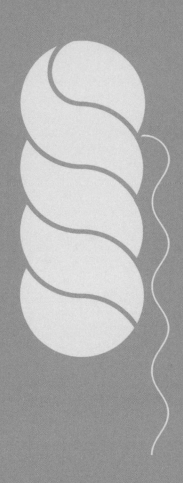

¿\¡/⁚/ ! \⁚\¡/;

lazy crafter

¿/!\⁚\ ¡ /⁚/!\¿

Tassel tie bunting

WHAT YOU NEED

- [ ] Whole balls or odds and ends of yarn
- [ ] 4mm (UK8:USG/6) crochet hook
- [ ] Scissors

This is the ultimate bits and bobs project if, like us, you can't bear to throw out even the shortest scrap of yarn. Don't those colours look sweet together? You can knock one of these up in an hour and it will make an awesome gift or a fancy trim on a wrapped present.

1 Make a loop, ch16, then cast off. Repeat this step lots of times. We made 90 of these little fellas!

2 Now tie your first chain piece in a knot at the top, making sure there is only a very small gap between ch1 and ch16.

3 Thread your next chosen colour chain length through the first and tie in a knot in the same way.

4 Continue in this way until you are happy with the length of your garland.

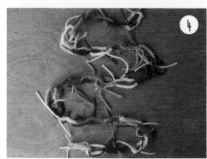

Tip! Play around with colours. Try layering up several lengths of garland when hanging to make a stunning feature.

Fancy tote bag

WHAT YOU NEED

- ☐ 50g balls of bamboo DK yarn in two colours (A and B)
- ☐ 4mm (UK8:USG/6) crochet hook
- ☐ Scissors
- ☐ Cotton tote bag
- ☐ Coloured craft pompoms
- ☐ Embroidery needle
- ☐ Embroidery thread

Jazz up a tote bag with this simple, bright crocheted trim. This is an excellent upcycling project and is a great way to reuse and reinvent any tired old tote bag. It would make someone a great gift, too.

Tip! This colourful tote will brighten up any dull grocery-shopping trip!

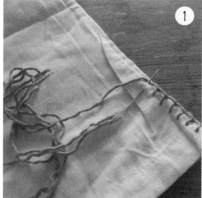

1 Using yarn A, sew in blanket stitch (see page 28) around the edge of your tote bag. This will form the foundation on which to work the crochet. Secure the sewing with a knot on the inside of your tote bag at the top.

2 Now make a slip knot with yarn B. Push your hook into the first blanket-stitch loop, place the slip knot onto your hook and slip through.

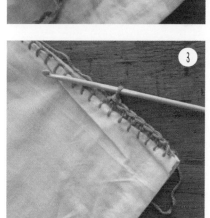

3 **Row 1:** Dc into every st sp along the whole edge of the bag (you will be working right to left).

4 **Row 2:** Cut yarn, then reattach it to first dc along base of bag, *make 11ch, miss 5dc, sl st into 6th dc; rep from * to end of base.

5 Cut yarn and sew in any ends to neaten. Lay out your craft pompoms to work out the best order.

6 Thread needle with sewing thread and attach your pompoms to ch6 in the edging. This should leave you with an even 5ch on either side of your pompom.

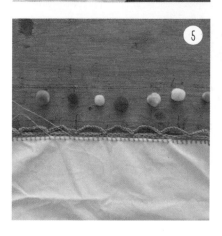

TEATIME TEA COSY, PAGE 78

FLOWER GARLAND, PAGE 62

Cord necklace

WHAT YOU NEED

- [ ] Small amounts of jersey T-shirt yarn in colour of your choice
- [ ] 9mm (UK00:USM/13) crochet hook
- [ ] Scissors

This project is speedy and seriously addictive! It is like the retro 'knitting Nancy' cord but without the doll and with some seriously chunky jersey yarn. We heart T-shirt yarn!

1   Make a slip-knot loop and make 3ch.

2   Keeping the working or first loop on your hook, pick up the next ch and crochet through to make another st on the hook.

3   Repeat this a third time. You will now have 3 active sts on your hook. This will look like knitting.

4   Now slip the two left-hand loops off the hook and pull the yarn through the right-hand first loop.

5   While securing the 2nd and 3rd loops from pulling out, draw the edges slowly together.

6   Pick up the loop to the left and pull the yarn through again.

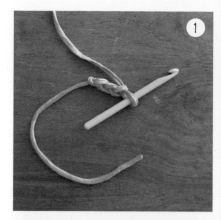

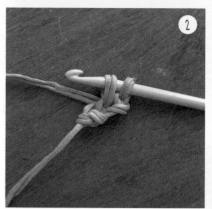

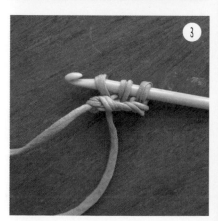

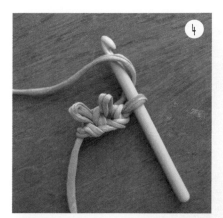

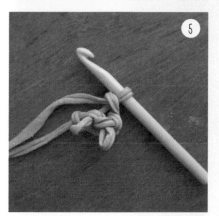

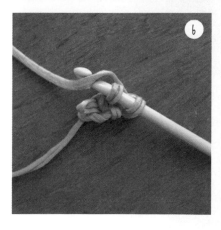

7 Finish the row by picking up the last
st and pulling the yarn through.

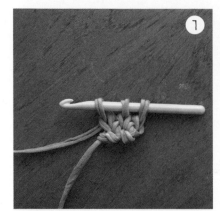

8 Repeat this sequence again and
again! Remember to take the
2 left-hand sts/loops off your hook
to begin as this pulls the yarn into the
cord, drawing the sides together into
a neat little tube.

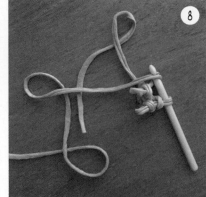

9 After a few repeats you will see the
cord forming.

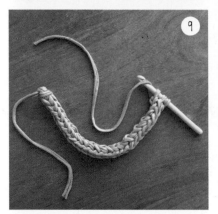

10 After 27 rows cut the yarn and pull
it through all 3 loops.

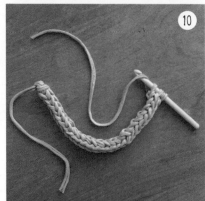

11 Slip the yarn through the last loop
to fasten off.

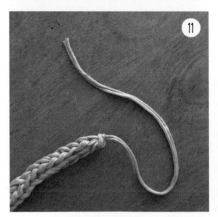

12 Tie the long ends together in a simple
knot to form the necklace. Why not
make one in another colour
afterwards to give to a friend?

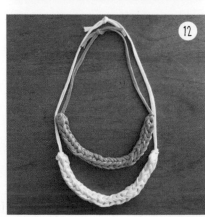

*Tip! Wear several cord necklaces
together and stagger their lengths
for a cool layered colour effect.
Perfect with a simple T-shirt!*

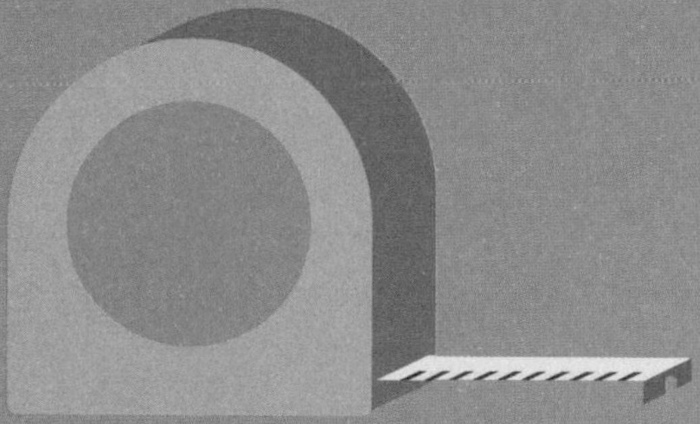

(`...` weeknight winners `...,`)

Block-colour coat hanger

WHAT YOU NEED

- ☐ 1 x 50g ball of chunky yarn in white (A)
- ☐ 1 x 50g ball of chunky yarn in green (B)
- ☐ 1 x 50g ball of chunky yarn in salmon (C)
- ☐ 6mm (UK4:USJ/10) crochet hook
- ☐ Wooden coat hanger
- ☐ Scissors
- ☐ Tapestry needle
- ☐ Measuring tape

Personalise your storage while being kind to your knitwear with this cool block-colour coat hanger. Not only will it brighten up your wardrobe, but the extra padding cares for delicate knitted items and stops any splinters causing unsightly snags.

Size

Length of coat hanger is 8½in (21.5cm). Crochet cover is 15¾in (40cm unstretched and 16½in (42cm) stretched; 3½in (9cm) wide. Measure your hanger to see if you need to alter the pattern to fit it.

Tension

10 dc sts and 7 rows to 4in (10cm) square using chunky yarn and 6mm hook.

Using yarn A, make 9ch.
Round 1: 1dc into 2nd ch from hook, 1dc into every st to end, make 1 turning ch (8 sts).
Rounds 2–10: 1dc into every st to end, make 1 turning ch.
Change to yarn B.
Rounds 11–30: 1dc into every st to end, make 1 turning ch.
Change to yarn C.
Rounds 31–50: 1dc into every st to end, make 1 turning ch.
Cut yarn and fasten off. Sew in all the loose ends.

Finishing

Push the hook of the hanger through the crochet fabric at the centre. Stretch your crochet around the coat hanger and sew from one end along the length to the other in a simple oversew stitch using your tapestry needle (see above).

Basket tidy

WHAT YOU NEED

- [ ] 2 x 50g balls of chunky yarn in colour of your choice (A)
- [ ] Oddment of contrast chunky yarn (B)
- [ ] 6mm (UK4:USJ/10) crochet hook
- [ ] Scissors
- [ ] Tapestry needle

Keep all your bits and bobs tidy and at the ready with a handy crocheted basket tidy or three. They can hang neatly from any hook or handle and make life much easier! Choose accent colours to go with your other accessories for ultimate craft chic.

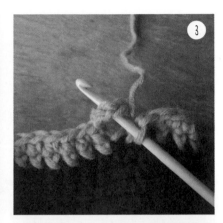

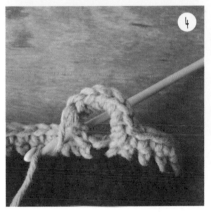

Size

4⅓in (11cm) tall x 4¾in (12cm) in diameter

10 dc sts and 12 rows to 4in (10cm) square using chunky yarn and 6mm hook.

1 Using yarn A, make 4ch and join with a sl st to form a ring.
   Foundation round: Work 9dc into the ring.
   Round 1: *2dc in next st, 2dc in next st, 1dc in next st; rep from * to end (15 sts).
   Round 2: *2dc in next st, 2dc in next st, 1dc in next st; rep from * to end (25 sts).
   Round 3: *2dc in next st, 1dc in next 2 sts; rep from * to last st, 1dc (33 sts).
   Round 4: Dc into every st to end.
   Round 5: *2dc in next st, 1dc in next 2 sts; rep from * to end (44 sts).
   Round 6: Shape base. Now picking up the inside half of the st, dc into every st to the end, creating a ridge on the outside edge of the circular base.

Rounds 7–17: Dc into every st.
Round 18: Cut yarn and change to yarn B. Dc into every st until you reach the start, ch6 to start your loop.

2 Sl st into first dc of last row to create a loop.

3 **Round 19:** Dc into every st until you come to 6ch again, then push your hook into the loop.

4 Work 6dc into the loop and sl st into first dc of last row.

5 Cut yarn and sew in ends on the inside using a tapestry needle.

Pompom plant hanger

WHAT YOU NEED

- ☐ 1 x 50g ball of chunky yarn in white (A)
- ☐ 1 x 50g ball of chunky yarn in grey (B)
- ☐ Yarn of your choice for pompom in two colours
- ☐ 6mm (UK4:USJ/10) crochet hook
- ☐ Scissors
- ☐ Medium-sized glass jar (we used a pickle jar)
- ☐ Pompom maker
- ☐ Measuring tape

Tip! Look at the back of the crochet and tail of your yarn to remind you where the new round starts.

Hanging your plants from ceilings and hooks around the home is a great way to save space and keep surfaces uncluttered. With our pompom plant hanger you can also add a pop of colour to any drab corner! So it can drain, your plant should be in a pot with holes and then placed inside the jar.

Size

7in (17.5cm) tall x 3½in (9cm) in diameter. Length of yarn to hang jar is 9in (23cm). Measure your jar to see if you need to adjust the pattern.

Tension

12 dc sts and 16 rows to 4in (10cm square) using chunky yarn and 6mm hook.

Using yarn A, make 4ch and join with a sl st to form a ring.

Round 1: 10dc into centre of ring, sl st to complete round (10 sts).

Round 2: Ch1 (counts as 1dc), *2dc into next st, 1dc into next st; rep from * to end of round, sl st to complete round (15 sts).

Round 3: Work as round 2, finish with 1dc into last st, sl st to complete round and cut yarn (22 sts).

Round 4: Join in yarn B, *2dc into next st, 1dc into next st; rep from * to end of round (33 sts).

Round 5: Continue straight into next round, *2dc into next st, 1dc into next 2 sts; rep from * to end of round (44 sts).

Round 6: 1dc into every st.

Round 7: Start shaping the base of the holder. With the right/neat side facing you, pick up the outside half of the next dc, cont in this way working 1dc into every st to the end.
Once this round is complete you will notice a small ridge.

Round 8: Go back to picking up both parts of the st and make 1dc into every st to the end.

Rounds 9–15: This next section is about building up the sides of your holder. Work the next 7 rounds by crocheting 1dc into every st to end.
Put your jar into the holder to check the size as you are crocheting.
Cut yarn and sl st into next free st to neaten the finished edge. Weave or sew in all loose ends.

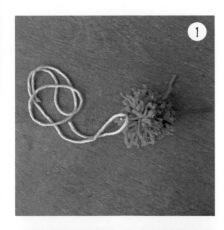

Finishing

1 Use a pompom maker to make two brightly coloured pompoms (see page 26). Cut 2 lengths of yarn A and, using your hook, thread this through the pompom and secure by tying onto a single strand.

2 Next use your hook to thread the length of yarn with the pompom on through the hole in the centre of the base of the hanger then back out through a stitch space to secure it.

3 Cut 3 lengths of yarn B and double them. Use your hook to pull them through three evenly spaced stitches on the finished edge of your plant hanger and tie a knot in the top.

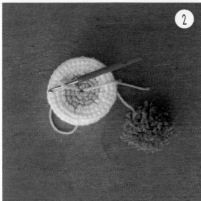

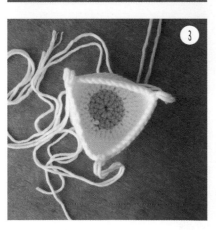

GRANNY SQUARE STOOL
COVER, PAGE 102

FANCY TOTE BAG, PAGE 38

Shell-trim placemats

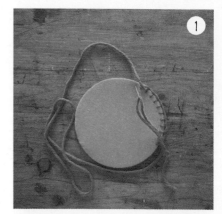

WHAT YOU NEED

- ☐ 50g ball of chunky yarn
- ☐ 6mm (UK4:USJ/10) crochet hook
- ☐ Round felt mats 6¹⁄₂in (16.5cm) in diameter
- ☐ Embroidery needle
- ☐ Scissors

Brighten up your dinner table with these fun shell-trim placemats. Making a nod to retro style but with contemporary colours, this is a great project for beginners. You can make smaller sizes for matching coasters.

Size

The round felt mats are 6¹⁄₂in (16.5cm) in diameter, although you can choose your own dimensions; 1 shell repeat is approximately 2in (5cm) long

1 Begin by sewing 40 blanket stitches (see page 28) around the edge of your mat (40 sts).

2 Continue around the entire edge and sew in your ends once finished.

3 Now work treble clusters for the trim. Join yarn to mat edge with a sl st to first blanket st sp.
Round 1: Miss 1 blanket st sp, 5tr into next blanket st sp, *miss 3 blanket st sps, 5tr into next blanket st sp; rep from * working this pattern all round the circular edge.
When you reach the end, sl st into last blanket st sp to join flat to mat edge and cut yarn.

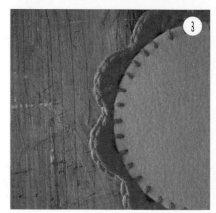

Tip! To space your 40 stitches evenly around the edge of your felt mat, fold the circle in half and mark the two opposite points using a pen or pins. Do the same to mark into quarters. Now use this as a guide to sew 10 evenly spaced stitches in each quarter.

56

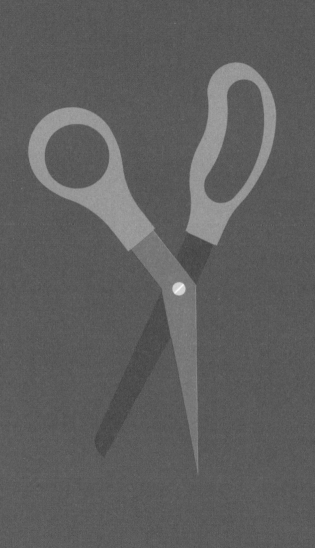

* < * > *

perpetual creative

* < * > *

Appliquéd pot holder

WHAT YOU NEED

- ☐ 50g ball of knitted tape yarn in colour of your choice
- ☐ Mercerised cotton DK (or finer) yarn for appliqué details
- ☐ 6mm (UK4:USJ/10) crochet hook
- ☐ 4mm (UK8:USG/6) crochet hook
- ☐ Embroidery needle
- ☐ Scissors

One could easily overlook the trusty pot holder, but for us they are a baking life saver, safeguarding digits from any cakey catastrophe in a stylish way. Traditionally made with thick cotton yarns, these little squares offer a tiny canvas for retro design. Adding an element of embroidery strengthens the holder by adding extra thickness while challenging your hand-stitching skills.

Size

6 ¾ in (17cm) square

Tension

11 dc sts and 12 rows to 4in (10cm) using knitted tape yarn and 6mm hook.

1 Using 6mm hook and tape yarn, make 17ch.
   Row 1: Miss 1ch, dc into every st through back of chain to end, ch1 and turn (16 sts).

2 **Rows 2–18:** Dc into every st to end, ch1 and turn.
   Break yarn.

For the edging

3 Change to mercerised cotton yarn and 4mm hook. Make a slip knot and sl st to join at any corner.

   Round 1: Crochet around the entire edge, picking up evenly spaced sts and working in a 1dc, 2dc sequence, working 3dc into each corner to help shape around the edge. At the same time, crochet in any yarn ends from the main body of your holder.
   Round 2: Dc into every st, stopping 3 sts before the end (this should bring you to the corner) ch15, miss 2dc, sl st to join to base just after corner. Cut yarn and tie in a firm knot.

4 Using chain stitch (see page 28), embroider the simple motif using the photograph as a guide. Sew the square first and then the central line. Sew in the ends neatly to finish.

Flower garland

WHAT YOU NEED

- ☐ Small amounts of chunky yarn in selection of colours
- ☐ 6mm (UK4:USJ/10) crochet hook
- ☐ Tapestry needle
- ☐ Scissors

Tip! This project is perfect for using up all the scraps of yarn you couldn't bear to part with.

This lovely flower garland is the perfect summertime accessory. Whether you use it to decorate your bike basket, adorn your hair, or hang it above your mirror, it is guaranteed to brighten up your day!

Size

1 flower is 2¾in (7cm) in diameter.
Row of 9 flowers is 8¼in (21cm) long.
Yarn onto which flowers are threaded is 17¾in (45cm) long.

1 Using your first colour, loop the yarn around your fingers once.

2 Push your hook through the loop, catch the long end of the yarn, then pull through the centre of your loop again (this does not count as a stitch).

3 Pull the short end of the yarn a little to make the loop slightly smaller and neater, yoh and make a ch st to close the large outer loop.

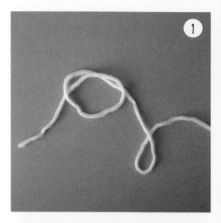

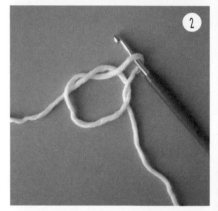

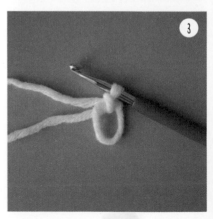

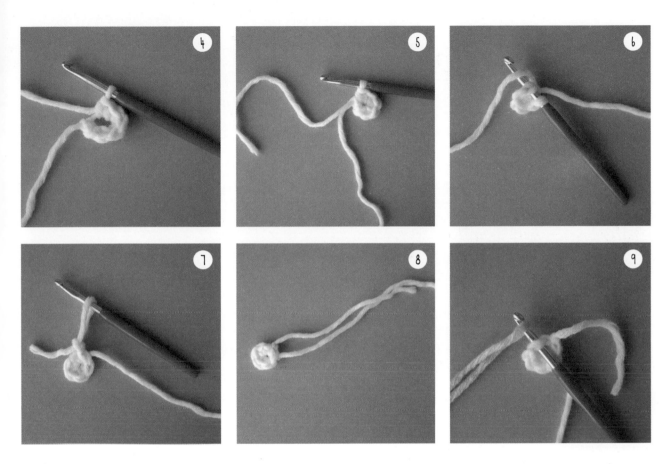

4   Work 5dc around the loop.

5   Pull the short end of the yarn to draw
    the loop and 5dc sts together into a
    small round crochet centre.

6   Sl st into ch1 to close the centre ring.

7   Cut yarn and pull through this last st
    to fasten off.

8   Your finished centre should look
    like this.

9   Push your hook through ch1 of your
    flower centrepiece and lay your
    second colour over hook.

*Tip! Keep your colours bright and contrasting. This makes the finished design lovely
and also helps you see what you are doing when crocheting into the centre piece.*

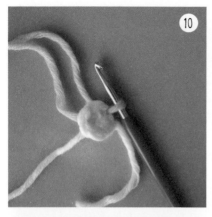

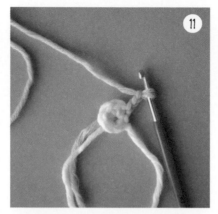

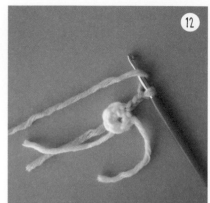

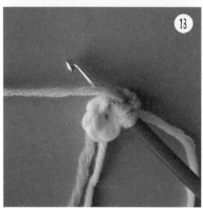

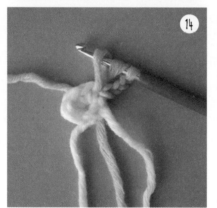

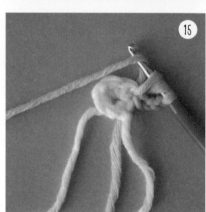

10 Pull yarn through ch1 of centre circle to make a loop.

11 Now make your first petal. Ch3 ready for first part of petal one.

12 Wrap your yarn over the hook towards you.

13 Push your hook into the same ch sp. You should have what looks like 2 loops on your hook at this point.

14 Wrap yoh towards you and draw a loop back through (make this the length of the 3ch) (3 loops on hook).

15 Wrap yoh towards you again.

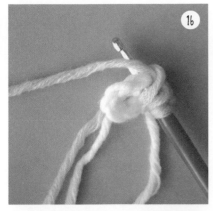

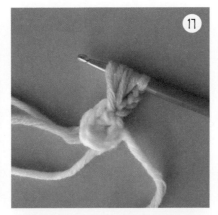

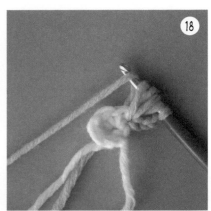

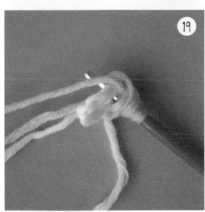

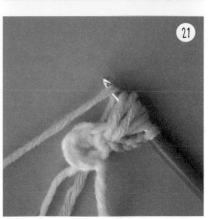

16 Push hook back into the ch1 sp.

17 Draw hook back through, pulling yarn with you to make next new loop on hook (make this the length of the 3ch) (5 loops on hook).

18 Repeat yoh towards you.

19 Push hook back into ch1 sp with yoh as before.

20 Catch yarn through st sp and draw back through (7 loops on hook) (make this the length of the 3ch).

21 Wrap yoh towards you again.

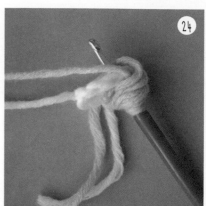

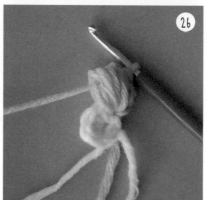

22 Push hook back into ch1 sp with yoh as before.

23 Catch yarn through st sp and draw back through (9 loops on hook) (make this the length of the 3ch).

24 Wrap yoh towards you again and push hook back into ch1 sp with yoh as before but for the last time.

25 Catch yarn through st sp and draw back through (11 loops on hook) (make this the length of the 3ch).

26 Wrap yoh towards you but this time draw through the loops on your hook.

27 Catch yarn and wrap it over hook towards you.

Tip! Keep all the petals the same height for optimum neatness!

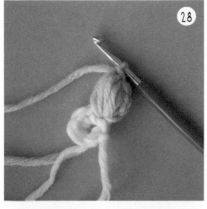

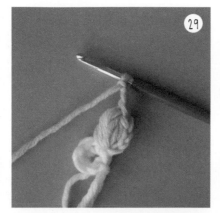

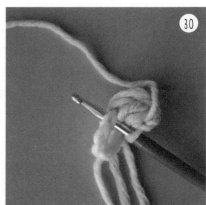

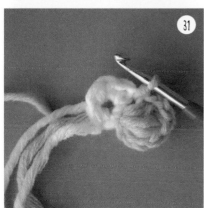

28 Slip through the loop already on your hook to pull the long loops together into the first petal.

29 Ch3.

30 Push your hook through the next st sp.

31 Sl st into st sp to close petal one (in new st sp). Now your first petal is complete, rep steps 11 to 31 a further five times, moving around the centre ring to make six petals.

32 At the end of petal six, sl st into st sp 1, cut yarn then pull through and fasten off. Use your hook to pull any ends through to the back of your flower and sew in neatly.

33 Your finished flower, on the right side, should look like this. Now repeat these steps and make nine more flowers. Use assorted colours – the brighter the better.

Tip! Time for a tea break!
Give those fingers a rest.

34 Thread your needle ready to join all the pieces together. You can use approximately 40in (100cm) of whichever colour yarn you have left over to do this. Turn your first flower over to have the back facing you; it should look like this.

35 Sew through the top centre part of one of your petals, picking up at least 1 full strand of yarn.

36 Next sew through the centre circle piece and back out through the petal directly opposite your first petal (that is, petal one and petal four).

37 Push your flower down towards the end of the length of yarn. Repeat this method a further eight times until all your flowers are lined up.

38 The finished garland!

Neon tablet case

WHAT YOU NEED

- ☐ 50 balls of chunky yarn in three colours (A, B and C)
- ☐ 6mm (UK4:USJ/10) crochet hook
- ☐ Scissors

Like a security blanket for your favourite gadget, this neon-striped tablet case is eye-catching and scratch-resistant! In this project you work your stripes in one direction so that the 'right side' can be extra stripy with a stitch ridge as well. We achieve this by working into the back loop only of the stitch so that the front gains the texture.

Tip! Bright and zingy! With this cover you'll never lose your tablet at the bottom of your bag.

Size

8in (20cm) x 10in (26cm)

Tension

12 tr sts x 6 rows to 4in (10cm) using chunky yarn and 6mm hook.

Special technique

See page 23 for how to work into back loop only to create a ridge.

1   Using yarn A, make 33ch.
    Row 1: 1tr into 4th ch from hook, 1tr into every st to end (30 sts). Break yarn.
    Row 2: Change to yarn B and sl st through ch3 sp to join to row below, ch3 (counts as first tr), *1tr into back loop only of st below; rep to end of row. Break yarn.
    Row 3: Change to yarn C, sl st to join to ch3 of row below, ch3, 1tr into next available st sp (work into back loop only of st), 1tr into each st to end of row. Break yarn.
    Rows 4–24: Rep this pattern working through colours A, B and C.

Finishing

2   Now it's time to sew in all those ends! On the back/inside of your crochet piece, use your hook to pull the cut ends through the fabric a loop at a time in the row of the same colour. Trim the ends.

3   Fold the left and right edges in to the centre and lay flat the first row against the last row. Sew along this edge in mattress stitch (see page 31), pulling evenly to join the edges neatly.

4   Sew along the bottom edge (this is the smoothest edge – the one without the turning chain sts).

5   Make a loop st in yarn C and slip it through the top edge of your case. Dc into next ch st, and then the following. In each band of colour you should be able to crochet 2dc into the first and second ch st of your turning chs; this will give you 44dc sts as your trim. Dc to end and break yarn.

6   Change to yarn B and dc into every st to end. Sl st to join to first dc and break yarn. The trim should be narrower than the body of your case to keep your tablet securely tucked in.

Tassel bag

WHAT YOU NEED

☐ Two cones of T-shirt yarn in contrasting colours (MC and CC)

☐ 9mm (UK00:USM/13) crochet hook

☐ Scissors

Combining two of our favourite things – crochet and tassels – this shoulder bag is the perfect size for all your essentials and is stylish to boot.

Size

Bag 8¼in (21cm) in diameter
Tassels approximately 8in (20cm) long

Tension

9 dc sts x 10 rounds to 4in (10cm) using T-shirt yarn and 9mm hook.

1 Using MC yarn, make 5ch and sl st into first st to join into a ring.
Foundation Round: Work 9dc into centre of ring and sl st to close.
Round 1: *2dc into next st, 1dc into next st; rep from * to last st, 2dc into last st (14 sts).
Rounds 2–4: *1dc into next st, 2dc into next st; rep from * working in spiral rounds (48 sts).
Round 5: 1dc into every st to end, sl st into next st to fasten off.
Repeat rounds 1–5 for side 2.

Tip! Getting to grips with working in the round is lots of fun with jersey yarn. Just remember not too pull too tight as it is super stretchy.

Joining

2 Line both pieces up on top of each other, wrong sides together. With your hook, pick up the inside half of one stitch on each side that sits directly opposite the other.

3 Still using yarn MC, crochet around the circumference of your bag pieces picking up only half a stitch from each side and working in sl st (inside).

4 Stop when you get to 6 sts away from closing the two sides completely. This will form your bag opening. Hook through to the inside of the bag and sl st to secure, then break yarn.

Making the tassels

5 Change to yarn CC. Cut 20 lengths approx. 24in (61cm) long and fold them in half. Insert your hook into the seam of your bag join and pick up one of the horizontal 'ladder' stitches. Place the fold of one of your tassel lengths onto the end of your hook and pull it through the 'ladder'.

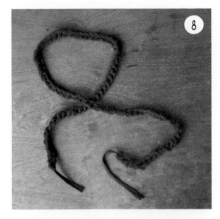

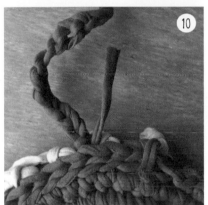

Tip! Using slip stitch to join your bag pieces securely is a speedy way to finish your project neatly!

6 Now hook cut lengths through this loop to secure the tassel to the bag. Repeat this process around the edge of the bag.

7 This decorative technique makes your handmade clutch bag just that little bit more special. Snip lengths down to suit your taste and add your last length centre top to close.

Adding the strap

8 Once you have completed your tassels, make a crochet chain for your strap, approximately 60in (150cm) long. This will make a sturdy over-the-shoulder or body-length strap approx. 35½in (90cm) long.

9 Use your hook to attach the strap to the bag body at the side where you joined the two pieces together. Hook the ends through from the outside of your bag to the inside.

10 You can now secure them by weaving into inside. We attached ours below the second tassel and used the uncrocheted yarn end to fasten it.

11 The finished strap.

MISMATCHED WRIST
WARMERS, PAGE 84

APPLIQUÉD POT HOLDER, PAGE 60

Teatime tea cosy

We all love a pompom, so why not invite your pals over for a much-needed tea break and wow them with your pompom-embellished tea cosy? Choose colours to match your kitchen, or make one as a gift – ideal for any tea party enthusiast!

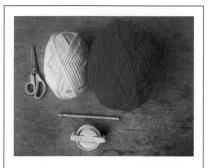

WHAT YOU NEED

- ☐ 2 x 50g balls of chunky yarn for cosy (A)
- ☐ 1 x 50g ball yarn of your choice for pompom (B)
- ☐ 6mm (UK4:USJ/10) crochet hook
- ☐ Pompom maker
- ☐ Scissors

Size

7in (18cm) in diameter; 8¼in (21cm) centre top to edge

Tension

5 tr sts and 4 rows to 4in (10cm) using chunky yarn and 6mm hook.

Special technique

When making a 3trpoof (also known as treble cluster), work only the first part of each tr st: *yoh, insert hook in next st, yoh, draw yarn through st, yoh, draw through 2 loops on hook; rep from * 2 more times, yoh, draw yarn through all 4 loops on hook to fasten together the tops into a 3trpoof.

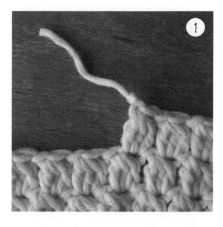

1 With yarn A, make 4ch and join with sl st to form a ring.
   Round 1: Ch3 (counts as first tr), work a further 12tr into the centre of the ring, join with sl st into top of 3ch (13 sts).
   Round 2: Ch3, 2tr into next st, 3trpoof into each of the next 2 sts, *ch1, make 1 3trpoof Into each of next 3 sts; rep from * to end, sl st to join.
   Round 3: Ch3, 2tr into next st (counts as 3trpoof), 3trpoof into each of next 2 sts, ch1, *make 1 3trpoof into each of next 3 sts, ch1; rep from * to end, sl st to join.
   Round 4: Work as round 3.
   Round 5: Ch3, make 1 3trpoof into each st to end of round. Do not sl st to join, just break yarn and fasten off.
   Spout and handle holes
   Round 6: Rejoin yarn to top of ch3 of previous round, ch3, make 1 3trpoof into each st sp 15 times, break yarn.

Tip! A perfect excuse to dust off your best china and invite friends over for a tea date!

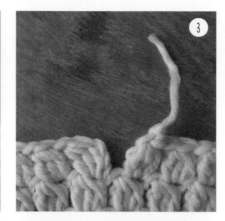

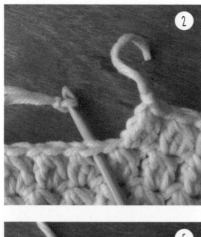

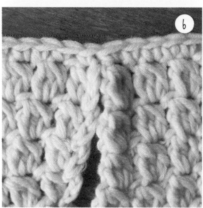

Tip! If you attach your pompom with a bow instead of a knot you can change the colour of your pompom whenever you like!

2   Rejoin yarn in next st sp.

3   Make 1 3trpoof into each st sp 15 times, break yarn.

4   You should see two separate sides with a space forming between them.

5   **Rounds 7–9:** As round 6.

6   **Round 10:** Rejoin yarn to top of ch3 of previous round, ch1, dc into every st to end, sl st into ch1 to join round. This will join the two openings together.
Break yarn and fasten off.

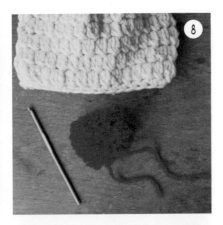

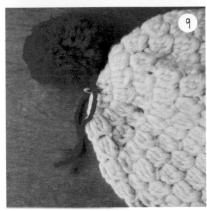

Adding the pompom

7   Now it's time to jazz up your tea cosy with a bright pompom! Following the steps in the techniques section (see page 26), use yarn B and your pompom maker to whip up a pompom in a colour of your choice.

8   You will need your tea cosy, hook and finished pompom.

9   Push your hook from the inside through the top of your tea cosy. Try to make sure it pokes through on one side of the starting round of your cosy. Catch one of the lengths of the yarn from your pompom and pull it through to the inside of your cosy. Repeat this step, pulling the second length of yarn from your pompom through on the opposite side of the top circle of your tea cosy.

10 Tie these two ends in a double knot to securely attach your pompom to the top of the tea cosy.

Squishy wrist rest

WHAT YOU NEED

- ☐ 50g balls of chunky yarn in three colours (A, B and C)
- ☐ 6mm (UK4:USJ/10) crochet hook
- ☐ Toy stuffing
- ☐ Scissors

Rest your weary wrists at your computer with this fun, boldly coloured wrist rest. Mix up the colour combos to match your workspace.

Size

17¾in (45cm) long x 3in (7.5cm) wide

Tension

12 dc sts x 10 rows to 4in (10cm) using chunky yarn and 6mm hook.

1 Using yarn A, make 14ch.
   Row 1: 1 dc into 2nd ch from hook, dc into every ch to end, ch1 and turn (13 sts).
   Rows 2–16: Dc into every st to end, ch1 and turn.
   Break yarn A and join in yarn B.
   Rows 17–32: Dc into every st to end, ch1 and turn.
   Rep this for 16 rows and break yarn. Join in yarn C.
   Rows 33–48: Dc into every st to end, ch1 and turn.
   Rep this for 16 rows and break yarn.

2 Working with a 12in (30cm) length of the same colour yarn as the stripe you are joining, use your hook to sew over and over from the start of yarn A to the start of yarn B, fasten off, change to yarn B and repeat.

3 Change to yarn C to finish the last part of your rest, making sure to leave the end open with a long enough length of yarn to finish.

4 Stuff with toy filling, cotton wool or the inside of an old pillow. Your rest needs to be firm but still squishy.

5 Use your remaining length of yarn and hook and close the end. Hide the end inside the rest and trim the yarn end. Then get ready to type your first novella!

Tip! If there's a bit of a breeze shooting under your door, you could always make a longer version of this and use it as a draught excluder.

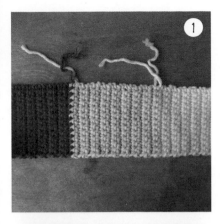

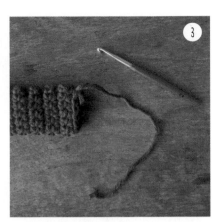

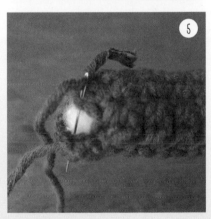

Tip! Sew through the gaps in your rows to keep stitch spaces even.

Mismatched wrist warmers

Size
6½in (16.5cm) long x 8½in (21.5cm) in circumference

Tension
12 dc sts x 13 rows to 4in (10cm) using chunky yarn and 6mm hook.

WHAT YOU NEED

- [ ] 50g balls of chunky yarn in three colours (A, B and C)
- [ ] 6mm (UK4:USJ/10) crochet hook
- [ ] Scissors

For wintertime adventures and cosy days away, these wrist warmers will keep your hands warm while letting you pick up that crochet project or climb a tree. Most practical, even if we say so ourselves! Mismatching your yarns will make them go further and add a quirky colourway.

Tip! Crochet over the yarn tail from the row below to fasten it in neatly as you go along. This will save fiddly sewing at the end.

1 Using yarn A, make 22ch and sl st to join into a medium-sized hoop.

Round 1: Ch3 (counts as first tr); now working into the back part of your ch, 1tr into every st (this will be one single strand) to end, sl st into top of ch3 of first 'stitch', break yarn.

Round 2: Join in yarn B. Picking up only the inside part of your st (that is, the right of the 2 strands), dc into every st to the end. This will make a ridged edge detail.

Rounds 3–11: Dc into every st, picking up both parts of the dc.
Cut yarn and fasten off.

Thumb hole shaping

Row 12: Rejoin yarn to st next to the one you just fastened off, ch1, dc into every st to end of row. (Make sure you catch all 22 sts otherwise you will begin a confusing internal decrease.) Break yarn and fasten off.

2 After a few repeats of this breaking yarn and rejoining yarn process, you will begin to see your thumb hole shaping up.

Rows 13–16: Rejoin yarn to st next to one you just fastened off, ch1, dc into every st to end of row, break yarn and fasten off.

3 Row 17: At the end of row 16 do not break yarn but go straight into row 17, bridging over your fashioned thumb hole and joining the sides together at the top to make a neat little thumb-sized opening.

4 Round 18: Break yarn and join in yarn C, ch3, work tr into every st to end, picking up only the inside part of your st as you did at the start to create a decorative ridge. Break yarn and weave in ends.

5 Repeat for the second mitten, changing the order of the colours.

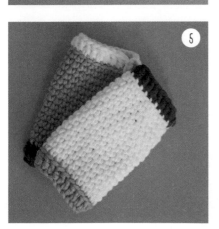

committed crafter

Brill bow tie

WHAT YOU NEED

- ☐ 1 x 50g ball of DK recycled denim yarn
- ☐ 4mm (UK8:USG/6) crochet hook
- ☐ 2 x plastic press poppers
- ☐ Embroidery needle
- ☐ Sharp-ended tapestry needle
- ☐ Scissors

This unisex accessory is a perfect outfit update for you or your beau. Made from recycled denim yarn, this bow tie is hardwearing with a wink to eco-chic. Pick your favourite colour to match your ensembles.

Size

12in (30cm) long; tie is 15¾in (40cm), centre piece is 3¼in (8cm)

Tension

22 dc sts and 22 rows to 4in (10cm) using DK denim yarn and 4mm hook.

Make the bow

Make 55ch (length should be approx. 12in/30cm).
Row 1: Dc into 2nd ch from hook, dc into every ch to end, turn and ch1 (54 sts).
Rows 2–14: Dc into every st, turn and ch1.
Break yarn. Sew in ends to neaten.

Make the neck tie

Make 72ch (length should be approximately 15¾in/40cm).
Row 1: Dc into 2nd ch from hook, dc into every ch to end, turn and ch1 (71 sts).
Row 2: Dc into every st to last st, then work 3dc into edge of turning ch on row below. Now work around the corner of the piece and dc into every st to end of the previous row, 3dc into end st and sl st to finish. You will have 2 rounded ends. Break yarn and fasten off. Sew in ends to neaten.

Make the central piece

Make 16ch (length should be approximately 3¼in/8cm).
Row 1: Dc into 2nd ch from hook, dc into every ch to end, turn and ch1 (15 sts).
Row 2: Dc into every st to last st, then work 3dc into edge of turning ch on row below. Now work around the corner of the piece and dc into every st to end/start of previous row, 3dc into end st and sl st to finish. You will have 2 rounded ends.

Tip! Crochet cotton is more rough and far less stretchy than other yarns so you might need to loosen your tension slightly.

1 You now have three crochet parts to assemble.

2 Fold in the left and right sides of the bow piece to meet in the middle, flat edges together. Using mattress stitch, sew top to bottom to join the piece into a tube.

3 Lay the central piece over the join and pull around the bow piece to form a bow shape.

4 Turn the work over and sew through the central piece using simple oversew stitches to secure the shape and pieces together.

5 Lay the neck tie piece on top of the central piece covering the previous sts. Sew through the neck-tie piece to the central piece to join all three pieces together.

6 Using your crochet yarn and a sharp-ended wool needle, sew one half of a plastic press stud onto the left-hand end of the neck-tie piece and sew its other half 1in (2.5cm) in onto the right-hand side piece. This is where they will overlap. Now sew the first half of the second press stud onto the end of the right-hand neck-tie piece and its other half 1in (2.5cm) in onto the left-hand piece. They will join and overlap. Your fancy bow tie is complete!

Chunky pouffe

WHAT YOU NEED

- ☐ Cones of T-shirt yarn in two contrasting colours (A and B)
- ☐ 9mm (UK00:USM/13) crochet hook
- ☐ Scissors
- ☐ Stuffing (we used the contents of two old cushions; you could also use toy stuffing)

This chunky pouffe is a homeware lover's must-have. Working with jersey T-shirt yarn, we opted for grey and pink, and we encourage you to be playful with contrasting colours. Make lots of pouffes in different sizes and colours and stack them up.

Size
41¼in (105cm) in diameter 4½in (12cm) deep

Tension
7 tr sts and 4.5 rows to 4in (10cm) using T-shirt yarn and 9mm hook.

Side 1
Using yarn A, make 5ch, sl st to first ch to join ring.
Foundation round: Ch3 (counts as first tr), 12tr into centre of ring, sl st into top of 3ch to join (13 sts).
Round 1: Ch3 (counts as first tr), 1tr into st at base of 3ch, 2tr into every st to end, sl st to join (26 sts).

Round 2: Ch3 (counts as first tr), 1tr into st at base of 3ch, 1tr into next st, *2tr into next st, 1tr into next st; rep from * to end, sl st to join (39 sts).
Round 3: Ch3 (counts as first tr), 1tr into st at base of 3ch, 1tr into each of next 2 sts, *2tr into next st, 1tr into each of next 2 sts; rep from * to end, sl st to join (52 sts).
Round 4: Ch3, 1tr into every st to end, sl st to join.
Round 5: Ch3 (counts as first tr), 1tr into st at base of 3ch, 1tr into next st, *2tr into next st, 1tr into next st; rep from * to end, sl st to join (78 sts).
Rounds 6–8: Ch3, 1tr into every st to end, sl st to join.
Break yarn and fasten off.

Side 2
Work rounds 1–5 in yarn B, break yarn and join in yarn A.
Work rounds 6–8 in yarn A.

Tip! Why not make two pouffes? One for you and one for your pet!

How to assemble

1 Make a loop and slip through any st sp to join.

2 Use your hook to sew over the edges through each stitch to begin to join both sides, picking up the same stitches on the opposite side to keep the edges evenly lined up.

3 Work in this way until you have 5–6in (12.5–15cm) left open.

4 Now stuff with toy filling or the contents of an old cushion.

5 Sew closed, break yarn and tie end with knot.

6 Push ends through to the inside to finish neatly.

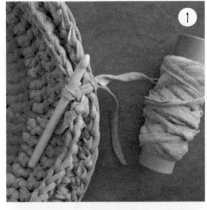

Chic string shopper

WHAT YOU NEED

- [ ] We used a cone of brushed crochet cotton found in a thrift store; you could also use 3 x 50g balls of fingering-weight crochet cotton
- [ ] 4mm (UK8:USG/6) crochet hook
- [ ] Scissors

Tip! Crocheting into the back of your foundation chain can be fiddly. Try to work with a looser tension when making your chain to allow for this. More room will make catching these little fellas easier and your finished tension neater.

Can you ever have enough shoppers? This lovely project is great for perfecting your chain and slip stitch technique and tension along the way and makes a mighty fine vessel for any juicy tomato or lettuce purchase.

Size

12½in (32cm) long x 10in (25cm) wide
Strap width 2cm

Tension

22 sts and 22 rows to 4in (10cm) using crochet cotton and 4mm hook.
NB: With this project we are using a hook larger than would normally used with this weight of yarn to give a more relaxed tension to the finished shopper.

The trim

1 Make 90ch, sl st to first ch to join into a big ring.
   Round 1: Picking up only the single strand at the back of your chain sts (instead of the two front strands; see page 25), dc into every st to end. This will give you a finished edge top and bottom and will prove invaluable when we get to joining our crochet net and adding the handles.

2 **Rounds 2–3:** Dc into every st to end, picking up both parts as usual. Do not break yarn as we will go into the net from here.

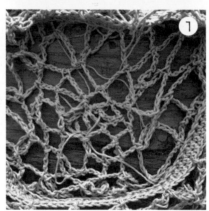

decreasing like this until end of round. Do not break yarn but cont crocheting around into next round in a spiral.

7 **Rounds 18–20:** Over these three rounds you will decrease and shape the bottom of the shopper in a more haphazard way but using the same 'ch5 and sl st into next space' method. If you are left with a gap at the centre of your shopper, ch 5 and sl st into the chain arc opposite to fill that space with net.

The net

3 **Round 4:** Ch10 and sl st into 5th dc of your next row working into the sturdy base you already have in place. *Miss 4dc, ch10, sl st into 5th dc; rep from * around the whole edge to end to finish with your first row of chained net. Break yarn.

4 **Round 5:** Make a loop and sl st to join around your first crochet chain length, *ch10 and sl st around centre of your next chained net arc (try to join roughly at ch5 to keep the net

spacing even and central – there will be some movement as we are not working into the chain, just around it); rep from * to end of round. Break yarn.
You will begin to see how the net is staggering.

5 **Rounds 6–14:** Rep Round 5 to form the main body of your shopper.

6 **Rounds 15–17:** Rejoin yarn with sl st, ch5 and sl st into next net arc, ch5 and sl st into the one after, cont

Tip! Make them in lots of different colours for all your many errands!

98

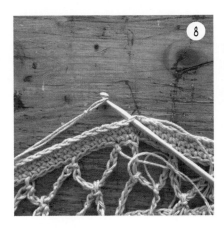

The handles

8 Starting on the trim band at the top, join yarn with sl st into the first free st sp after where you began. Make sure you have the right side towards you.

9 **Round 1:** Dc5, ch30 to shape handle, miss 15dc on crocheted edge and sl st back to join, dc30 to take you around to next handle space, ch30, miss 15dc and sl st to join into dc16, dc to end.

Round 2: Dc15 into trim, *dc30 into back sts of handle ch (giving a neat edge on both sides),* dc30 into trim, rep from * to*, dc15 into trim to end of round.

Round 3: Dc into every st (including handles) to end, sl st to join round, break and fasten off yarn (you should end at 15dc past handle).

Finishing

10 Turn your bag inside out and tie a double knot in each of your yarn joins and cut ends to ¼in (6mm). Don't waste time sewing in yarn ends for this free-spirited project.

TASSEL BAG, PAGE 72

NEON TABLET CASE, PAGE 70

Granny square stool cover

WHAT YOU NEED

- [ ] Lots of different colours of chunky yarn; you can use new balls or leftover bits and bobs
- [ ] 9mm (UK00:USM/13) crochet hook
- [ ] Stool
- [ ] Scissors

Our granny square-covered stool is a colourful and on-trend interiors update for any cosy kitchen or craft room. Combining techniques introduced earlier in this book we take our crochet skills to the next level in this playful project. There is no set order for your colours, so go wild with mismatched row striping.

Size

15¾in (40cm) square

Tension

3 tr st clusters and 4 rows to 4in (10cm) using chunky yarn and 9mm hook.
Note: With this project we are using a hook larger than would normally be used with this weight of yarn to give a more relaxed tension to the finished giant granny square. This allowed us to fit the square over the stool top easier.

1   Using your first colour, make 3ch and join with sl st and make a loop.
    Round 1: Ch3 (counts as first tr), 2tr into centre of ring, ch2, *3tr into centre, ch2; rep from * twice more, sl st into top of 3 ch to join. You should have four clusters of 3tr sts bridged together by 2ch that form your corner spacing. Break yarn.

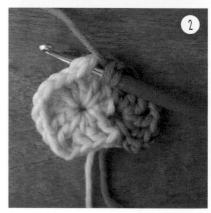

2   **Round 2:** Change to your next colour, make a loop and push hook through the ch/corner sp closest to your cast-off tail. Place your new colour loop onto the hook and slip through to join new colour to square. Ch3, then work 2tr into this corner sp to make first of two tr clusters.

3 Ch2 (acts as corner spacing) and 3tr into same sp. Each corner will have two tr clusters to make the angle.

4 Place your hook into next corner sp, *3tr, ch2, 3tr (there are no ch sts between the clusters on the flat sides, only between corner clusters). Rep from * twice more to end of round and sl st to join at top of 3ch.

5 **Round 3:** Start as before and sl st next colour into corner sp to join. (Ch3, 2tr, ch2, 3tr) into same space = first corner cluster. Place your hook into next sp, *3tr. There will only be one cluster repeat in this side space. Move your hook into the corner ch sp and work 3tr, ch2, 3tr; rep from * to end where you will have four corner double clusters and four side single clusters.

6 Round 4: Starting at corner, work as Round 3 adding an extra single cluster between each of the corners. (Corner, 3tr into next sp, 3tr into next sp, corner.)

Rounds 5–13: Rep this pattern of shaping your corner with 3tr, ch2, 3tr then working single clusters into each of the next side sps. (Corner, 3tr into next sp, 3tr into next sp; rep as many times as it takes to work along the side; corner.) Break yarn and fasten off after round 13.

Use hook to weave in any cut ends you have missed.

Lay your giant square neatly on top of your stool with the corner points lined up, right side facing you. To attach the crochet piece we are going to weave around the edge of the entire square with our hook picking up every 3rd st.

7 When you get to the corner, hook your yarn through the central space in the corner of the row below. Later on we will tuck this pointy corner underneath out of sight.

8 When you have woven all the way around your square and back to the start, tie a half knot and pull the ends, drawing the crochet fabric to fit around the square base top of your stool. Tuck all four pointy corners underneath the main body of crochet and out of sight. Tie again to secure tightly.

9 Snip the ends down and tuck up.

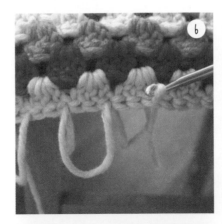

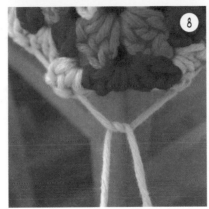
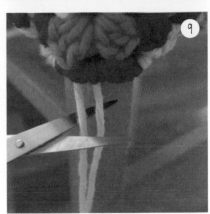

Tip! Another traditional name for the granny square is Afghan square. So now you can wow your pals with technical crochet lingo!

Trendsetter turban

WHAT YOU NEED

- ☐ 2 x 50g balls of chunky yarn in cerise
- ☐ 6mm (UK4:USJ/10) crochet hook
- ☐ Tapestry needle
- ☐ Scissors

This uber-cool turban will get you through autumn to winter in style, harking back to the 1920s and icons such as Clara Bow.

Size

8in (20cm) from front to top; 15in (38cm) from front centre point over top to back centre point

Tension

12 tr sts and 6 rows to 4in (10cm) using chunky yarn and 6mm hook.

Special technique

To work into back loop only, the hook is inserted only into the back loop (the part of the stitch farthest away from you) instead of through both of the loops. This has the effect of creating a ridge (see page 23).

Tip! Chunky yarn is perfect for this project. Your finished turban will keep you warm and chic all winter round!

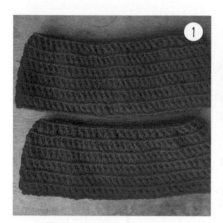

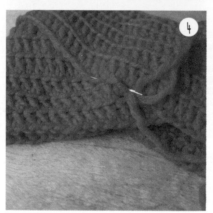

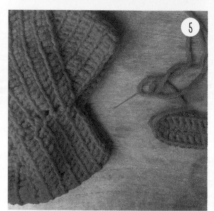

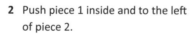

1   Make 70ch and join with a sl st into
a large loop.

Round 1: Ch3 (counts as first tr), tr
into every st to end of round, sl st
to join.

Round 2: Rep Round 1 but this time
and going forward crochet into the
back loop only of the st to create a
ridge textured pattern.

Rounds 3–5: As Round 2.

Round 6: Ch3, miss 1 st, *tr into next
4 sts, miss 1 st; rep from * to end
making a small decrease and shaping
the piece.

Make another piece the same.

*Tip! Keep your join neat by
sewing into the row edge of
your turban pieces. The stitches
will be instantly camouflaged
by the finished edge.*

2   Push piece 1 inside and to the left
of piece 2.

3   Sew through the stitch edge to join
the two overlapping areas together
with a running stitch.

4   Follow the edges around to close
both top and bottom side seams,
leaving you with only an opening
at the top.

5   For the top piece, make 16ch, miss
2ch, tr into next ch, tr into every st
to end, tr4 into last st to work around
the end. Tr into every ch all the way
back along the underside of your tr
row to beg of work, sl st into ch3
to join.

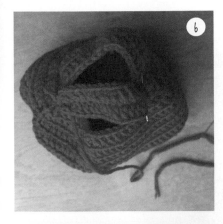

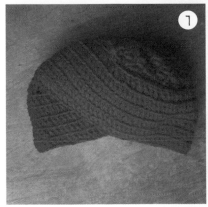

Attach the top piece

6 Lay the top piece over the opening lengthways parallel to the front overlap detail. Pin at the end opposite to where you are going to begin sewing to keep it even. Sew in same running stitch method as used when joining the main body pieces, working in a clockwise direction. Fasten off inside and trim the ends.

7 Voilà! Super-stylish and super-cosy.

Vino holder

WHAT YOU NEED

☐ Cones of T-shirt yarn in two contrasting colours (A and B)

☐ 9mm (UK00:USM/13) crochet hook

☐ Scissors

This cool bottle holder helps you to get to that party or picnic with wine safely in tow! We have combined bright stripes and vertical weaving to achieve an on-trend plaid pattern. For this project, the brighter or more contrasting the colour combination, the better!

Size

9½in (24cm) long x 3½in (9cm) in diameter

Tension

6 dc sts and 8 rows to 4in (10cm) using T-shirt yarn and 9mm hook.

Special technique

To work into back loop only, the hook is inserted only into the back loop (the part of the stitch farthest away from you) instead of through both of the loops. This has the effect of creating a ridge (see page 23).

Main part

1   Using yarn A, ch4 and sl st to join into a ring.
    Foundation Round: Work 10dc into centre of ring.
    Round 1: *1dc into next st, 2dc into next st; rep from * to end (15 sts).
    Round 2: Shape base: dc into back loop only of every st. This will pull the yarn into the right position to work in the round all the way up to the top.
    Round 3: Dc into every st (picking up both loops of st), sl st to join, break yarn.
    Round 4: Change to yarn B, dc into every st to end, sl st to join, break yarn.

Round 5: Change to yarn A, dc into every st to end, sl st to join, break yarn.
Round 6: Change to yarn B, dc into every st to end, sl st to join, break yarn.
Rounds 7–15: Change to yarn A, dc into every st to end, sl st to join, break yarn.
Use your hook to weave in the cut ends.

Woven plaid detail

2   Cut 2 lengths of yarn B approximately 39in (100cm). Starting at the top and as a single strand, weave the yarn running stitch fashion in a straight line to the bottom edge of the piece.

3   You don't have to go through the whole thickness of the crochet; you could just pick up the top part of the dc st, making sure your weaving is evenly spaced.

4 Repeat the row with the second half of your length of yarn, staggering the first stitch that you weave through at the top so that the whole length doesn't pull out. Let the long ends hang at the bottom edge until you have finished the second and then the third rows. The second row is spaced approximately ¾in (2cm) to the right and the third another 1⅝in (4cm) to the right of that.

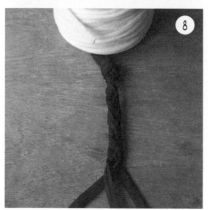

5 Once you have finished your weaving and are happy with its spacing, loop the long ends back over the edge/fold of the base of the holder and inside, then pull them all out again through the central hole in the crochet base.

6 Knot all six ends together as close to the crochet as possible and trim down to make a tassel.

The strapping

7 Cut six 60in (150cm) lengths of yarn A, split into two lots of three, and knot each at the very end.

8 Place the yarn cone on the end of your length to hold fast while you braid (or ask a friend to hold it if there is someone nearby!). Braid, keeping the tension firm, then tie off close to yarn ends. Repeat this for both braids.

9 Take your first braid and weave it into the very top row at the opening, miss 2 st sps and weave back out. Repeat this until you have woven right back to the start of your row.

10 You will now be able to pull this like a drawstring to make sure your bottle is safe and secure.

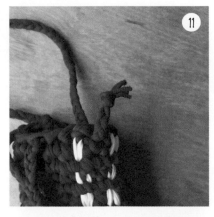

Tip! The thick crochet will keep your wine cool, so all you have to worry about is which cheese to bring along to the party!

11 Now make a carrying strap with the second braid. Push the knotted end of the braid through the first row from the top (inside to outside).

12 Knot the ends once, pulling tight and stretching the yarn to make sure it is extra secure.

13 Knot a second time and repeat on the opposite side of the circular rim.

14 You now have a useful wine bottle holder complete with handy strap.

15 This will keep your beverage safe and sound as it accompanies you to any party or picnic.

····· **bits and bobs** ······

Conversions

Crochet hooks

Metric (mm)	UK	US
2.00	14	-
2.25	13	B/1
2.50	12	-
2.75	-	C/2
3.00	11	-
3.25	10	D/3
3.50	9	E/4
3.75	-	F/5
4.00	8	G/6
4.50	7	7
5.00	6	H/8
5.50	5	I/9
6.00	4	J/10
6.50	3	K/10½
7.00	2	-
8.00	0	L/11
9.00	00	M/13
10.00	000	N/15
11.50	-	P/16

UK and US crochet terms

UK	US
Double crochet	Single crochet
Half treble	Half double crochet
Treble	Double crochet
Double treble	Triple crochet
Treble treble	Double triple crochet

Resources

supplies

Amazon
www.amazon.co.uk

C&H Fabrics
www.candh.co.uk

eBay
www.ebay.co.uk

Hobbycraft
www.hobbycraft.co.uk

Ikea
www.ikea.com

Prym
www.prym.com

Tiger
www.tigerstores.co.uk

Wool and the Gang
www.woolandthegang.com

events

Craft Hobby & Stitch International
www.chsi.co.uk

Creative Stitches
www.creativestitchesshow.co.uk/
glasgow

Hobbycraft Show
www.hobbycraftshows.co.uk/
birmingham/autumn

Knit Out and Crochet
www.craftyarncouncil.com/
knitoutandcrochet.html

Knitting & Stitching Show
www.theknittingandstitchingshow.com

MADE Brighton
www.brighton-made.co.uk

inspiration

Craftgawker
www.craftgawker.com

Craftivists
craftivist-collective.com

Design Sponge
www.designsponge.com

Golden Hands magazines
Look out for copies at flea markets, thrift
shops or second-hand book shops

Heals
www.heals.co.uk

Henry Holland
www.houseofholland.co.uk

Knit the City
knitthecity.com

Pinterest
www.pinterest.com/supersuperhq

Shauna Richardson
www.shaunarichardson.com

Wool and the Gang
www.woolandthegang.com

Everybody's grandma in the 1970s!

Acknowledgements

We are so happy to see the Super+Super series continue to grow and provide such inspiration to all you crafty people out there. It really is a joy for us to see everyone making these ace projects. We'd like to take this opportunity to thank each and every one of you for buying this book. You are personally responsible for making our dreams a reality.

We'd like to thank all our friends and family for supporting us through this venture and for listening to us talk about these books for hours on end. You really are super.

We'd also like to thank our cats for providing us with hours and hours of comfort and attention.

Index

To order a book, or to request a catalogue, contact:
GMC Publications Ltd
Castle Place, 166 High Street, Lewes,
East Sussex, BN7 1XU, United Kingdom
Tel: +44 (0)1273 488005
www.gmcbooks.com